# Contents

**02** A Great Idea

**06** Getting Started

**10** Time Out With God

**13** In a Nutshell

**15** Going Deeper

**19** Pass It On

# A Great Idea

*To become a Christian is to begin a relationship.*

John 17:3 says, 'Now this is eternal life: that they know you, the only true God, and Jesus Christ, whom you have sent.' It is a relationship built on knowing and being known by God. He loves you and desires your love.

## What?

God's genuine desire and pleasure is to be with you. He endured the cross for that sole purpose, so that you might experience his love now and forever.

## Each and every day, God is longing to show you his love.

By spending regular time with him – talking, listening and learning – you will grow to know him and his love for you, and to live your life for him.

The Song of Songs is an Old Testament book that describes the intimacy of marriage but also paints a beautiful picture of Jesus (the Lover) and those he loves (the Beloved).

Reflect on the words of the Beloved in chapter 7:10-13.

Notice the joy and expectancy of the Beloved, looking forward to time with God. They will experience the vineyard's beauty together, the new growth, the delight of sweet fragrance; they will enjoy new discoveries and reflect on old memories.

SONG OF SOLOMON 7:10-13 (NIRV)
WORDS FROM THE BELOVED:

*'I belong to you, my love.*
*And you long for me.*

*Come, my love. Let's go*
*to the country.*
*Let's spend the night in*
*the villages.*

*Let's go out to the*
*vineyards early.*
*Let's go and see if the*
*vines have budded.*
*Let's find out whether their*
*flowers have opened.*
*Let's see if the pomegranate trees*
*are blooming.*
*There I will give you my love.*

*The mandrake flowers give*
*off their strong smell.*
*All the best things are*
*waiting for us,*
*new and old alike.*
*I've stored them up for*
*you, my love.'*

3

# Being with God is all that matters.

*'I am the vine; you are the branches ... As the Father has loved me, so have I loved you. Now remain in my love.'*

John 15:5, 9

## Why?

In John 15, Jesus compares our relationship with him to the connection between a vine and its branches. He repeats one phrase 10 times: 'Remain in me.' It means 'Make your home in me.' Home is a warm word for most – a place where we feel comfortable, welcomed and able to be ourselves. Jesus gave up everything to make a home with us.

Quality time with Jesus takes us into that intimate, secure and joyful place – to be 'at home' with him. We hear his loving voice and fear disappears (1 John 4:18). Closeness to Jesus helps us to go deeper with him.

## How?

Maybe you know a Christian you admire – someone who has been walking with God for a long time, whose life has been transformed by him and whose love for him is infectious. What is their secret? Is it all the sermons they've heard, books they've read or events they've attended? Not necessarily.

Most would say that growth has come through the ordinary, everyday decision to spend personal time with God in prayer and in his word. This has become their way of life and it has shaped everything about who they have become.

As Hebrews 5:14 shows us, maturity comes with time.

The aim of this booklet is to provide you with a tool to help you regularly spend time with Jesus and record what he shares with you.

*'Solid food is for the mature, who by constant use have trained themselves to distinguish good from evil.'*

Hebrews 5:14

*Take the time for this adventure! Let's begin...*

5

02

# Getting Started

*How can you make this work for you? A few tips...*

Make a mug of tea, coffee...

Have a Bible, notebook and pen handy.

Choose a place without distractions. See how it goes for a few days and, if need be, choose again.

Don't recline or lie down. Sleep will stalk you! Choose your favourite chair or sit at a table.

# 1 — Start small

It is easy to assume that you should begin with an hour a day – after all, you are meeting with God. But 10 minutes is enough to begin with. Let it grow naturally. As you become more comfortable with Jesus and develop your relationship with him, you will find that you want to spend more time with him.

# 2 — Create the environment

Most of us have a lot going on in our lives already, so finding space for time with God may be a challenge. Try to find a time and place where you can be alone and away from distractions. Many prefer the morning, as it can be easier to carve out time before the world rushes in and the day's busyness fills our minds. However, mornings don't work for everyone, so look for a time and space that suits you and your life stage.

# 3 — Choose the passage

The choice is yours, for 'all scripture is God-breathed and is useful' (2 Timothy 3:16). It does, however, help to have a plan. If you follow a regular Bible reading plan, you can choose one section for each day. You might want to read a Gospel (Matthew, Mark, Luke or John), then a New Testament letter (Romans through to Jude) and intersperse it with a few Psalms. A Bible Reading Plan can be found at: www.navigators.co.uk/reading-plan.

Over time, God will speak to you from every part of his word. Even when you revisit well-known passages, he will have new lessons for you. Hebrews 4:12 says, 'The word of God is alive and active.'

# 4 — Keep a journal

Recording what you have learned will help you understand and remember what God is saying.

Here are some pointers on journal writing:

☐ *Make it simple*
You don't need to impress. What matters is meeting God. Write it whichever way suits you. For example, some people journal their thoughts as a stream-of-consciousness prayer to God; others prefer bullet points, jotting down thoughts without forming sentences.

☐ *Make it a staple*
Try to write in it every day, even on days when you feel 'blah'. Meeting with God on 'ordinary' days helps us deal with life more successfully. When we miss it, we have missed out on what God might have said. Record the date as well, so that you can look back in years to come.

☐ *Make it into a soundbite*
Finish by writing a summary thought or prayer to take into the day. Some days he will remind you of familiar thoughts, other days he will show you new ones. Ask God to give you an opportunity to share something of what he's said to you, too.

*A journal is there to serve you, not a rule to burden you.*

# 5 — Go exploring

We are all uniquely made by God, so as you spend time each day with Jesus, feel the freedom to explore. Look for the ways that best enable you to receive from Jesus.

Always ensure that the word of God and prayer are at the centre of your time with him, but feel free to introduce things that help you to focus and engage with him.

Here are some ideas to try:

- Sing, write or listen to a song.
- Use different translations of the Bible.
- Read a prayer or poem.
- Draw a picture or annotate a passage.
- Set out a candle or sit by a beautiful view.
- Rewrite a passage in your own words.
- Go for a walk.
- Emphasise different words as you read a passage.
- Ask new questions – Saul asked Jesus, 'Who are you, Lord?' (Acts 9:5) and the answer changed his life!

# 6 — Pause to review

At the end of each week, take time to review, reading through your thoughts and prayers. It can be easy to forget what God has taught you.

You may find that God has been speaking to you on a similar theme for a number of days. It would be easy to miss this if all you focused on was one day at a time.

Try to summarise the things that God has been saying. Spend some time thanking and praising God.

# Time Out With God

*'It seems, in fact, as though the second half of a man's life is made up of nothing but the habits he has accumulated during the first half.'*

FYODOR DOSTOEVSKY

# W

## WELCOME God
1 MINUTE

Pause to recognise the one you are meeting with. Enjoy a warm welcome from the God who loves you and longs to spend time with you, however you're feeling today. You might like to start with a song or verse that reminds you of what God is like. You could use the words of a psalm to praise him, such as Psalm 143:8:

'Let the morning bring me word of your unfailing love,
for I have put my trust in you.
Show me the way I should go,
for to you I entrust my life.'

*What other things would help you pause and know Jesus is with you and for you?*

# A

## ASK God to speak
5 MINUTES

Read something from the Bible slowly and thoughtfully (10-15 verses). Ask God to show you his heart. Ask him to share something with you that you can reflect on today. Take your time, reading the verses over and over.

Note down your thoughts in your journal.

*Do you have a sense of how Jesus is asking you to respond today?*

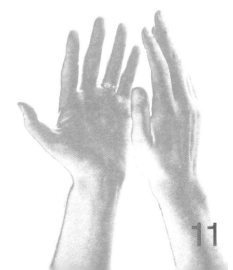

# I

## INVITE God into your day
3 MINUTES

Reflect on what will happen over the next 24 hours. Is there something you're dreading or looking forward to? Invite God to help you with what is hard and thank him for what is good. Invite God to meet your needs and the needs of those around you. Use the thoughts from your journal.

Are there things you're holding on to from yesterday? Invite God to forgive you and guide you into this fresh day, as you hold on to his unfailing love.

*Remember that nothing is too insignificant to bring to Jesus.*

# T

## TAKE God's word with you
1 MINUTE

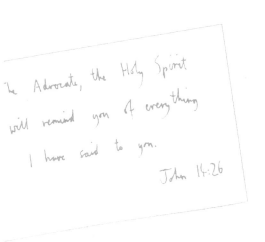

The Advocate, the Holy Spirit will remind you of everything I have said to you.
John 14:26

Look at what you've written in your journal. Summarise the key thought into a simple prayer, word or verse.

Write it in your phone or on some paper and carry it with you. Look at it from time to time during your day and think and pray about it. Ask the Spirit to help you, for Jesus says, 'The Advocate, the Holy Spirit ... will remind you of everything I have said to you' (John 14:26).

*How will you keep leaning on Jesus today?*

12

# In a Nutshell

*Take time to WAIT expectantly before God each day:*

**W** — **WELCOME God**
PRAISE

**A** — **ASK God to speak**
PONDER

**I** — **INVITE God into your day**
PRAY

**T** — **TAKE God's word with you**
PERSEVERE

# Going Deeper

## As you Welcome God, learn to PRAISE

*There is great power in praise.*

There is great power in expressing our love and thanks to our Father God.

When King Jehoshaphat led out his army to fight, he organised men to march in front, singing praises to God (2 Chronicles 20:20-26). When the army reached the battlefield, God had already destroyed the enemy.

Praise and thanksgiving are like weapons from God, which have divine power to help us fight against sin in our lives and evil in our world (2 Corinthians 10:4). As you notice something about who God is or how he loves you, turn it into praise. You'll be surprised at how this practice affects the way you approach the rest of your day.

# 'Oh, how I love your law! I meditate on it all day long.'

Psalm 119:97

## As you Ask God to speak, learn to PONDER

Meditation is an essential part of a growing relationship with God.

Unlike other forms of meditation, which seek to empty the mind, biblical meditation is about filling your mind with God's word.

As you meditate, new truths will be revealed, new lessons learned and a deeper relationship with Jesus will develop. The Holy Spirit may also use illustrations, pictures, songs or poems to help you understand his word.

There is a good illustration of meditation in nature. A cow consumes 30 to 70 lb of food a day, but it then sits there for hours, chewing, to get the most out of all that food. Meditation is like that. God's word is rich with meaning and as you 'chew' on what he has said to you, it influences your heart and life.

### How do I meditate on scripture?

Read the words slowly and notice what stands out.

Check out different Bible translations.

Ask questions:

- 📖 What does this show me about who God is?
- 📖 What does this show me about who I am?
- 📖 What does that word mean?
- 📖 What would it be like to experience this first hand?
- 📖 How is the Lord inviting me to respond?

15

## As you Invite God into your day, learn to PRAY

God is always ready to speak, but listening takes time.

Life is busy. We rush from one thing to another. It is easy to rush through time with God as well, telling him our needs but not pausing to listen. King David once wrote, 'In the morning I lay my requests before you and wait expectantly' (Psalm 5:3).

God told Moses he wanted to meet with him. So, 'When Moses went up on the mountain, the cloud covered it, and the glory of the LORD settled on Mount Sinai. For six days the cloud covered the mountain, and on the seventh day the LORD called to Moses from within the cloud' (Exodus 24:15-16). Moses sat there for six days in silence. Many would have given up and missed what came next: 40 days and nights of glorious time with God.

God's Spirit lives within you and as he speaks, prompts and guides, you'll learn to recognise his voice.

### Top tip

When God speaks, things happen. He makes and keeps his promises. He gives new insights. But our brains can be like sieves! It is important to record what God tells you. Later on, you will be able to look back and see his faithfulness.

*Waiting quietly in God's presence is deeply rewarding.*

## As you Take God's word with you, learn to PERSEVERE

Let me encourage you to make careful plans to keep regularly taking time with God and taking God's word with you. Make sure you have set it as a daily priority.

It can be easy to lose momentum when you enter a new season, when you finish the book you're reading or when you skip a day or more – and the enemy does not want you to make time for this. Be ready to try out different options and simply begin afresh. The Spirit is ready to help you.

Travelling this journey alongside someone else will make all the difference. Tell a friend what you're doing. Ask if they would pray for you and ask you how it's going. Perhaps you could encourage each other in this. As Hosea 6:3 reminds us, this is not a solo venture, and together we can rely on God's persevering love.

*'Oh, that we might know the LORD! Let us press on to know him. He will respond to us as surely as the arrival of dawn or the coming of rains in early spring.'*

Hosea 6:3 NLT

17

# Pass It On

*We are blessed to be a blessing.*

It may be that what God shows you in your time alone with him isn't just for you (1 John 1:3). Ask God if there is a soundbite of your discoveries about him that he wants you to share with someone else. You will be surprised how often this happens.

Look for opportunities to share what your relationship with God means to you, too. You could share that it is built on knowing and being known by the God who loves, that it takes time to develop but it's worth it, that it includes talking, listening and learning, and then living out what God tells you to do. It is the greatest of adventures!

# Help others begin their journey

*Here are three ways you could use this booklet to help someone start taking time out with God...*

## 1

### Give it away

Once you have established your own regular routine, you could pass the booklet on to someone you think it could help, or have a few copies available to give away.

## 2

### Use it to show the way

As a member of Christ's family we can have the privilege of passing on what we are experiencing every day, and it is so easy to get others started.

Here are some simple steps...

- Invite someone to meet with you and give them the booklet to read.

- When you meet, read a short Bible passage together and ask God to meet with you in this time.

- Take two or three minutes to reflect on the passage individually, asking, 'Who are you, Lord?' and, 'What shall I do, Lord?' and jot down what comes to mind.

- Take two minutes to share with each other what you heard God say, then thank God for meeting with you both.

- Agree to do this on your own each day for the next week, then meet up again to share how the Lord met with you and share another time with him together.

# 3

## Use it as a group

This is also something you can do if you meet as a small group of friends from church during the week. It only takes a short time, but it can lead to a lot of mutual encouragement.

# ...another adventure begins!